How to Digital Detox

By Hitachi Choparazzi

Acknowledgements

I'd like to give all due praise to the Creator of the universe and life spirit itself. My GMa Lawson, Mama Lisa, my kids Jr., Pierre Kydale, Kylan, and beautiful intelligent daughter China. All my NYC, Midwest, Down South & West Coast family & friends/fans. To all the youth and generations to come who take the time out to read this Digital Detoxification book to take a digital vacation, to find themselves, learn, grow, and reconnect with reality, environment, and true innate nature. Love y'all. Bless!

ATTN:

This book is a non-fiction work of art through the author's perspective as a digital analysis, which is an examination of things to determine its parts or elements. Then comes up with his own conclusion of the facts, data, research, etc., to work better and effective solutions offering, teaching advice, and problem solving methods to all who would like to take practice in daily detox remedies and effective solutions. Pragmatism.

However, the author is in no way promising you instant detox from the digital space. Nor instant gratification. This book is solely created to help teach you, make you aware, and help you to take effective steps in your life to self-digital detox. Something you have to want for yourself to put in the time, work, effort, self-discipline, and energy towards your detox daily practice. Therefore the author is not liable for your digital detox. Intentions is to offer this book as a tool to teach, problem solve, add value, break habits, and detox. Also get you back to human nature basics, not digital dependent.

Contents

FOREWORD

You can miss some of the most precious moments in life, games, sports, family, etc., being on edevices. Caught up in the VR movement, missing the moment.

It's a digital zombie apocalypse worldwide and crisis. We must get our real identity back, versus our digital identity of false digital augmented perceptions and false senses.

Who has the problem? What is the problem? Who has the power and responsibility?

Turn off all notifications and put mobile devices on airplane mode to help you take an initial step from being distracted and pulled back to edevices and those top 10 apps you cannot live without in your daily ritual of virtual reality and social media norms. In order to recognize your habit and patterns of consumer electronics binge, first in order to solve, and withdrawal in time stipulations, to avoid neglect and problems from your real-world life, work, and loved ones.

I will show you how to take a step back before you had internet access, apps, and edevices to think and act for you. With nothing and that time and space of your life where you actually had human nature, and your sensory as main tools and guidance. Most of all your energy source and willpower to your health, exercise, eating habits, and work performances. To utilize time precisely, not fruitlessly.

It's time to digital detox and awaken from being a digital zombie in the digital matrix of this new digital consuming era. The digital data doesn't show you how to detox or have the algorithm for it. We're so reliant on our smart devices versus our smarts, willpower, memory, and work ethics. It's all about instant gratification and convenience versus delayed gratification, which is the mid-brain addictive cues of neurotransmitter to the synapse and dopamine overload of euphoria effect, same as an addictive drug that amplifies the sensory and stimulus organically. Hacking instant reward and gratifications.

I will show you effective solutions, cause and effects, methods to detox, and problem solve all your troubleshoot digital areas.

- Chapter 1 -

"New Era Digital Norms"

Welcome to the new millennium with the introduction of the new digital era of consumer electronics. It is called the digital takeover.

This includes new social digital norms, virtual reality, augmented reality, A.I. (artificial intelligence), and a data-driven marketplace. All to the global digital consumers of all ages, genders, creeds, and backgrounds. A future technology digital wave.

A lot of people disconnected from the real world, life, work, family, and responsibilities because of new digital world distractions from what truly matters the most. Consuming too much time indulging in fruitless areas.

It is a new era of instant gratification, convenience, on demand, binge watching, and indulging in next big edevice, causing everyone to be super-sensitive and censored in every aspect. We live in a world of filters without having true filters on self or digital space usage and addictive behavior patterns. Lost in the digital matrix, eyes glued, hypnotized.

We are digitally distracted. The subconscious makes no distinction between the inner and outer. It is time for a thorough process of digital detoxification.

How to recognize habits, patterns, and addictions. How to reverse them with effective solutions and detox daily practices as a new ritual. How to get your kids off YouTube and tablets. How to get off social media and stop scrolling. How to stop using dating apps and top 10 apps you really think you need. How to stop sweating your emails, spending way too much time on emails even if you have work-based. You must limit your time and be careful not to hang out in your emails. Also if you struggle with game apps or porn addictions. Addiction psychologist cannot help with this or prescribe insomnia meds. You suffering from insomnia, sleep deprived because you're phone-struck in a digital consumer world. The digital zombie in the digital matrix.

We must detox! Get back to our human nature and sensory naturally.

Detox, noun: Detoxification from an intoxicating or addictive substance.

Detoxify, verb: To remove a poison or toxin or the effect of such from; 2) to free from addictive or intoxicating substance or from dependence on it.

First you must hold yourself accountable by recognizing or admitting you have or do spend way more time than you should online, binge watching, or on mobile devices. People will validate your excessive edevice usage if you're in denial. Fall victim to it. Could be causing major damage in homes, relationships, neglect, or not paying attention to loved ones. Poor performances at work, inattentive on projects. No growth and digital effect of the new world norm holding you back from your true life course and tap into your fullest potential of self and the universe all around.

Texting while driving, which could be fatal and extremely dangerous, more than drinking and driving. People, teens constantly put their life on the line over a simple text message that takes 4.6 seconds to check, which average person don't have enough self-discipline to wait or even pull over on the side of the road. Instead they further engage, and put other people, communities, and commuters in jeopardy of harm's way. It's not pride or being selfish, it's simply called digital addiction with addictive visual cues. Health concerns, neck problems, and future chronic eye problems, etc.

We do not daydream no more or have daily vision boards of goals either because we are too busy being digital robots. On auto-play and automated victims to being over-consumed by digital world and lying dormant in the digital space.

Each day globally someone leaves their child or pet in the car, distracted. However, they will not forget their mobile phone or edevices. Since when did a digital device matter over human life or a pet that's alive and actually breathing? That's how inflicted we are amongst this new digital wave era. Innocent people, kids, and pets are victims of neglect and constantly out in harm's way because of all these digital distractions and shorter attention spans. A goldfish has a 6second attention span, a second more than the average human and especially digital consumer, which is 5 seconds for a human, excluding being on edevices checking notifications, social feeds, and texting constantly.

This is the digital dilemma we face daily that has become the new era digital norms. Some people don't even notice the switch in themselves, energy, household, or workplace.

Magnified to the screens daily for extensive hours on end. If you do not detox, it can be highly detrimental sooner or later.

Nowadays people too lazy to cook, clean, or know how to take care of personal hygiene. Neglect everything they know and own, looking for the fastest results and instant gratification being all about convenience on demand. Further spoiling and feeding your chemical dopamine of addiction in your mid-brain thru the reward system going berserk with visual cues and hacks, over-indulging in quick hacks for mental, physical, and digital stimulus.

It's true we write the programs and program the machines. Now we are letting the machines program us and too reliant. We becoming too dependent on apps, A.I. doing all our thinking and storing memory for us, versus our own short-term or long-term memory storage.

If you ask 10 people and 10 kids what's their grandmother or mother's phone number, they would tell you hold on and look in their contacts under the name, then retrieve the actual 10digit number to call. Studies showed 1 out of 10 adults would actually remember by heart, whereas 2 out of 10 kids would memorize it. The kids only because they did not have an actual mobile device they owned.

A.I. (artificial intelligence) will be the next 15 to 20 percent future jobs automated, putting people out of jobs, cutting labor cost. Most people in what they think is the picture-perfect ideal career path. However, they are too digitally consumed to even see this problem exists, and refuse to evolve with future boom and a digital marketplace.

3.4 billion people have internet home access, double that on their phones and edevices. 6,000 new apps come out a day. Digital natives, also known as young people, consumers a third of internet use.

A lot of digital natives and millennials is not aware of automated process or data being the new oil. Automate is new, tech, and electricity. Automated is future way and wave, but people don't embrace or take advantage of opportunity of the big technology shift. It was meant to automate your business or workplace methods, etc. It was key to find A.I. ways that's smarter to cut cost or work and automate it. Do 10x your level, then do it cheaper than anybody. Instead we get sucked into the new digital consumer wave to wipe out, lost.

Data is precious and the new wave of sourcing directly. It cannot be no automated service without data. Data-centric assets, data-centric monopoly business, also social media platforms control data, buy data, and hoard it. They all use it to better business and products to determine new status quo or break the status quo with a new algorithm. Data is used to sell to big investor companies and research for business. They collect from people ways, habits, likes, engagement patterns, and personal things or privacy. Even your niche products thru SEO (search engine optimization). Merging companies use it, too.

They breach your data and consume it without your permission or user's consent to the apps or platforms. However, most of us are hypnotized by the digital consumer matrix to be aware of the data trade or that the data crisis even exists and that they are victims of data-centric quotes daily and make up algorithms of data.

It is data accessing stores and the traffic content, how long they were at the location, what time most people frequent the location, etc., all from a satellite in orbit. Then they take that collected data from people and sell it to big VC (venture capital) firms. Again, we must detox to be aware of the total wave before you become more digital data with no rights retained like you do not matter.

In this book of digital detox I show you how to detox and break out of patterns and habits. Then you will be able to get your personal identity back versus your digital profile identity. Teaching you how to think, reconnect, and be aware. Push them back into reality, accountability, and challenges to detox recovery process. Learn new methods to deal with digital distraction to focus back on real life, sustainability, and development that needs to be in those broken or troubleshoot areas.

We need to further engage in human social interaction and outdoors, too. The environment is meant to soak up and fresh air, sunshine to fuel your energy and body. Indoors glued to our screens and edevices makes us fatigued, sluggish, causing health problems where we dependent on supplements and 15-minute workout hacks to make up for all of our digital space usage. Not just blinded but addicted in denial. Even all our natural brain functions and sensory stimulus is being neglected and shrinking rapidly. If we not still using it, we definitely losing it, deteriorating millions of cells in lightning speed. Don't continue to feed digital false senses.

An epigene is created and it's a trait that you develop like certain addictions and passed down to kids or grandkids. So we must be and think divergent. Have a filter to detox. If not our future generations will be lazy and further consumed of our passed-down pattern traits, which in the family if one person does it, so do the rest, and true for the nation and globally affected.

Thru the internet the world is being brought together and right to your fingertips and face. Also technology to allow you to reach every point of earth and space in an even shorter time. We see ourselves faced with great challenges, influences, consumer electronics, pressure economy/, threatens to continuously choke us.

How can we emerge from the fog of digital consumer era and powerlessness? It's only a mistake if you don't learn from them. After you have moved yourself back from self-destruction to a place of awareness, make the paradigm change and look for new possibilities. Simply direct your attention away from the problem/usage and fix it on the solution and detox.

Can it be that our reality is the direct result of our conditioning, thought pattern, type of awareness, and self-discipline? Apparently the cause lies in the effect on the material and digital realms.

- Chapter 2 -

"Edevices, Social Media, & Gamers"

A new edevice drops every month, forcing people to keep up with the wave of latest and greatest technology and not optimizing or prioritizing. The digital world has divided us from our divine perfection and self.

It's about who has the latest and greatest devices, or more cameras and higher speed on mobile devices, 4G versus 5G. It's indirect consumer electronics competition wars. The phone is your actual identity now versus your personal identity, giving a false sense of reality

You are judged on what type of phone you have or type of services, and the actual carrier, too. Poor people sit outside in line for days to buy new expensive mobile device, even if it sets them back with financial priorities, irresponsible.

People will suffer from emotional distress from not having a phone or the latest new phone or not being able to pay their bill. Once they lose WiFi or cannot pay for WiFi services, without WiFi people and the youth transform into a withdrawal state like an addict or go into a state of depression and anxiety transforming mood swings. It alters people's moods, which extremely matters in your everyday life choices and mental health.

Mobile and digital devices are number one most addictive, more than coffee, drugs, vaping, alcohol, sex, etc. People text versus talk while in the same room/place or household. Don't poison your home or next generation with helping capturing them furtherance in digital captivity handheld hypnosis devices, handicapping sensory natural stimulus.

Sensory cells will signal your brain and connect with brain nervous system cells. The back of your brain is visual cortex. Your sense organ is a bodily structure as an eye or ear that receives stimuli as heat or light, which excites neurons to send information to the brain. Sensational is arousing an intense and usually superficial interest or emotional reaction. Finally sensation is awareness as of noise or a mental process as of seeing and hearing due to stimulation of a sense organ, an indefinite bodily feeling or a condition due to excitement. The thing that causes this now is all quick hacks of virtual reality, digital era, and augmented reality being superimposed. It's not natural no more that way it's becoming out of control and consuming us, and our natural human behavior and nature habitat. So your social skills you lose and natural senses and chemistry amongst human nature and traits. They diminish more and more.

I wanted to first educate you on your natural sensory and how they work and stimulate.

Virtual reality is an artificial environment that is experienced through sensory stimuli as sights and sounds provided by an interactive computer program. Also the technology used to create or access a virtual reality.

Anterior cingulate cortex (ACC) is decision making based on reward values, but also generate new actions based on past rewards/punishment. Insular cortex (IC) attaches consciousness to body, impaired with empathy, etc. The orbital frontal cortex assets value. Then we default choices. People will steal and rob for phones and edevices, all from these digital addictions locked into your mental and neurotransmitters.

We began to see and act how we are neurological wired thru our perceptions. People are more infatuated with their Surface Pro versus being interested in their own pro-life management. We become so convenience oriented, if we don't have a certain device, app, or internet we go berserk. You let your phone automate you and your algorithm versus its algorithm off your data usage, habits, patterns, apps, and social platforms. A.I. is programmed for it all.

We become steadily stuck in virtual reality as our own physical reality. Augmented reality superimposes things on your screen which hacks into your mid-brain to signal dopamine receptors, further feeding your addictions and stimulating sensory hacks that's all digital generated, not naturally. So we become continuously dependent on sole digital world and shift our mind frame, altering our sensory organ.

It gave everybody their own means to be heard and have their own reality show, turning into their perceptional superstar. A false reality of perception and based on created perception of ego and digital footprint or an influencer impact globally.

Now people focus solely on digital personality and picture-perfect profile for digital validation. People cannot stop recording, commenting, or wanting to be seen with more social likes and views with validated social feeds.

You must identify primary field of interest, personal development, and prolific quality output and control. We know from quantum physics that consciousness is the decisive factor in creating a reality out of the cloud of possibilities.

However, no more self-filter, accountability, just chasing streams/clout, and trying to go viral and trend at any cost for notoriety. Existing in the mind only, imaginary and unreal, but they still crave it and chase it in awe. Struck given to foolish or fanciful moods or ideals, whimsical, with the act or result of curving and bending reality and engagement, false presentation.

A lot of people on social platforms cannot engage in real interaction or call only 1 or 2 real friends in case of a true emergency to help them in real-life scenarios from their social media friends and followers. Some people actually believe that all those followers and friends is their actual friend out of a digital space, with a false sense of reality fallen victim of the digital takeover. Really offline those same people would not even reach out or acknowledge you in person. Maybe even possibly deny being your friend on social media platforms.

It's not about a million dollars nowadays with digital natives. Its importance is about a million likes or views that's weighed at more value to them versus an actual million dollars do. Which is clearly a false augmented version of reality.

Social media profiles and picture-perfect imagery trying to maintain an impeccable digital footprint at all cost for public eye and peer pressure, or sibling and classmate rivalry of digital identity and virtual reality imposed. People say how they feel unfiltered blurted out on tweets and comments without thinking, purely off of impulse. Including public shaming, trolling, or cyber bullying, all because of the digital persona they transformed into behind the screen, not scenes. Whereas, people actually believe they can superimpose every thought good or bad, hurtful or devastating, regardless of the effective negative on a human being's life, feelings, livelihood, or emotional state. They become super-villains trolling to the supercomputer that has their mind lost, stagnated in the digital matrix hypnotized. They will all still tell you to this very day they are fine, feel fine, and actually deny they have a problem and this exists.

Peer-to-peer interaction be aware of social norms that sway and influence you to go with the majority and false wave of social media reality. Also be aware of digital footprints, the ones you create on a cyber or social media space.

Who we are is who we physically rehearse and our action. Everything based on digital formats is simply tools and not for you to overindulge fallen victim of it into a digital zombie, which could be the lead cause of stress. You must keep mobilizing energy and true nature. It's not hard to heal and repair. Detox from internet and try out real social engagements.

In order to keep your peace and sanity, you need a break from social media platforms, apps, and games, including your top 10 most used apps. Fight off temptation and avoid temptation triggers. You must focus on power of self, the mind, body, spirit, thoughts, actions, words. Not focus on battery life power of the phone or edevice.

All the new viral challenges are new waves of movements that has become part of cyber culture norms. A lot of digital natives and millennials do these challenges to be seen versus the cause. Making their cyber debut with hopes to go viral and trend with their auditions to all challenges. Challenges is not a bad thing, it's just when you doing every and all challenges on the web to be seen and chase clout, seek viral validation, it's a problem. You need to admit to snap out of it first to be able to detox from it all around.

Finally, the next issue we will tackle and shed light of another area to digital detox is gamers. Gaming apps or gaming consoles are the number-one most addictive in digital space for the digital native, second is social media platforms. The average digital native gamer spends more than 8 hours a day, whereas recent poll showed that millennials spend 12 hours gaming, which is all way too much time. That's half a day excluding sleep and work hours if employed. Clearly something, someone, or yourself is getting neglected without no true disregard. By gamers abusing the gaming digital system, they let go of personal life and enter into a virtual reality and augmented reality world. This addiction also fuels your visual cues and signal dopamine chemicals to reward system. People even use gaming apps while driving and at work on the job, breaking main focus and affecting work performance. It produces insomnia more than social media induces insomnia.

Once gamers indulge and enter into this gaming space and platform, they are consumed by the next 2.0 version of the latest game or gaming system. They are influenced by gaming community and peers to compete on being the best rank at all particular games always, chasing levels of a top-ranking performance.

People play globally and made it into esports and rivalry gaming beefs, comps, and chasing tournament prize money along with bragging rights and name going viral. It is nothing the matter with extensive time in gaming if it is your primary source of income and occupation, not just a mere hobby you have since a kid where it became a life habit versus work skill.

Some gamers love the games, action, social digital interaction that they do not have or experience in the real world. They use it for escape reality tool, but often get stuck in the gaming matrix. Others they have a negative and reverse effect where they become the game and act out on real life stage and can be detrimental or a public safety threat with mass shooting rampages after it draws you in without sleep, days in and out, it starts to trigger and alter your ego and perceptions and can actually warp your mind. Also give you a false sense of reality hacking into your sensory organs, too. This is the part that most gaming console of actual games and apps warn you about addiction and spiral effect of negative augmented reality reversed gone wrong to the 33 percent gamers mind it taints daily. It should be aware, cautious warning labels, but they want you to continuously buy and be digital gaming consumers. Must be aware of usage and gaming effects don't slip out of reality. Later I will address this issue how to detox from it.

- Chapter 3 -

"Digital Zombie Apocalypse"

In the first chapter we address the problem. The second chapter we tackled the cause. This third chapter we will talk about the effect, which is really an inevitable after-effect like a digital epidemic disaster.

This after-effect hypnosis is now a digital zombie apocalypse. People are actually hypnotized to their edevices, eyes glued to screen or strapped to their faces like goggles. Texting while driving, neglecting self and others, not eating or exercising. Picking up bad habits and following into perpetual digital patterns. Oblivious to the hypnosis or that a digital paradigm zombie apocalypse exists. It's personal habits and digital social habits. Your strengths and core shapes mood, health, and happiness. However, with virtual reality, augmented reality hypnosis, we alter mood, health, and happiness.

There are no unhealable people, only unhealable effortless people with no initial push to correct their wrong actions, habits, and patterns. It's not an unhealable illness, it's your unhealable innate nature switch that you choose to leave shut off with every excuse in mind. To be healed means to recognize wrongs and to commit to the works to right and award it. To be complete because when we sick, we lack something, our trust and will. Must first be clear on what it is and the cause you are trying to heal first. Clear vision, intention, and habits give and patterns show that, too. High performers seek clarity always for success and best results.

Perhaps digital devices and virtual reality technology has programmed our subconscious? Have you zombified, glued, and consumed. The driving force behind our actions is our subconscious, and we or some social digital norms has pushed, triggered, or programmed it. Now even digital downloads have us used to automated mode. We are shrinking memory hippocampus further, getting stuck in digital zombie mode and digital dependent instead of being independent. It was meant and designed for us as a tool, but not for us to become a pro-tool and consumed with digital addiction with detrimental behaviors. Only thing that counts is what you believe and see in yourself—self-image counts.

You must stop making excuses. The common denominator of failure is excuses. It's the center point of failure. It don't make you a bad person, but you can be making bad choices and creating patterns while making bad habits, too. The excuse is poison. Catch excuses and stop them from being frozen and paralyzing you. You don't want to be in freeze mode in a digital zombie apocalypse. It's no excuses or giving excuses for people to justify their digital abuse or usage for their actions.

An example is if you show 10 people an even amount of wedding pics and funeral pics, depending on their actual mood, they will tell you what they seen more of. Of course the person in a negative environment or mood would say they seen more funeral pics, whereas the upbeat person with positive vibrations and outlook will say they seen more wedding pics, according to the London university study. The same goes for if you are trying to warn a smoker that smoker causes cancer, and a person next door just died from lung and throat cancer. They will say because the guy was an old man, and they still have many years left to quit, or they just only puff on them and don't inhale the smoke in too long. They will deflect and make all the excuses up in the world to justify their actions or plan of action. This is the same exact outlook people have for this digital era wave. They simply laugh when you or a loved one calls them a digital zombie and suffering from digital denial and abuse of overload usage, which leads to neglecting everything else in your life circle.

Instant gratification causes digital natives and millennials to need and like self-recognition and pat on the back. They don't have steam to get going or stop cold turkey, especially when it's automated and an easy digital system set-up and convenient for them. They don't manage their time wisely into beneficial essence versus personal gratification. Delayed gratification is priceless and key because you will retain it longer, also helps to reprogram your reward receptors and sensory false digital stimulus.

You must manage your digital space usage time and weigh if it's really important or for personal play, habit, or pattern. You cannot train yourself. Training is a behavior modification. You are teaching yourself new habits and patterns, not training yourself. Teaching is more therapeutic and when you learn new habits, your subconscious picks it up and makes it into pattern and a reality. Also develop that trait.

Energy is always great when it's higher. Keep good energy to do good in your learning and detoxification process of new human nature habits of self. You will continuously be successful and break digital status quos and social norms habitual patterns of falling into a digital zombie, the digital apocalypse. It will move you to keep a daily detox ritual.

Push yourself and people to digital detox and move the needle. Without progress it's not growth or true change of imbalance. Protect your standards and challenge yourself to avoid temptation triggers, visual cues that stimulate your sensory and fuel dopamine synapse receptors. You can influence, persuade, impact, and inspire others to detox digitally and seek change for betterment versus further engaging in the digital stick matrix web of zombie consumers.

Kids deal with rejection, irritability, social withdrawals, hyperactive, and disengage in school works. Their attention span is lost in the digital space, too. It's hard for them to learn simple things. They cannot focus and concentrate on what is being taught to them due to their young minds being distracted and burnt-out from tablets, binge watching, and video games, becoming part of the zombie digital.

The parents are to blame, but do not truly know they are at fault because they are too busy digitally consumed and installed automated programs in them and household. Parents do not actually realize it or see the neglect. You can let social media platforms, tablets, video games raise your kids. Then send them to school to figure things out like everything will be okay. It's way more pressure on the teacher and classrooms. Teachers are too underpaid to teach and play psychologist to each individual student daily. Parents must engage with kids' schooling and interact with them after school and work hours. They monitor their children when they are babies, but soon as they hit preschool, first thing the parents do is hand the kids a tablet.

Which further enables the kids into a digital world that spirals with hypnosis. Parents forget kids are like little sponges that soak everything up from their parents. Parents forget they are the leaders and mistake it for liability and responsibility. It's not just child safety and taking care of them with clothing and food. You influence, impact your children and household. The parents set a tone. Kids absorb habits, patterns, and traits. Also energy, dysfunction, etc., and reciprocate that at school, online, or indirectly.

Parents are automated digitally and they automate their kids indirectly, creating digital kid zombies, too. Kids need all nature human traits and sensory developments, outdoor space and people interaction to help with their engagement people skills and boost their immune system. If you live in a digital boxed-in life from your smart phone, smart home, to your electronic car, how will your child ever step out of that to build immune system strong against diseases and viruses that you had at the same age as your child?

Now we are forced to self-detox and digital detox our kids and households. The youth is the truth and our future. We do not want to create more artificial intelligence in our children. We do not want our kids dependent on devices, apps, and technology to do everything for them.

You want all your kids to be successful and independent on self. However, most kids cannot cook, clean, fish, memorize phone numbers, or do manual problem solving without Google help. Most kids spend far less time outside and way more time on tablets, mobile devices, or game consoles. Kids are fastest phone typers. Kids ages of 10 to 19 text 10 words more than adults. Two thumbs are better than one finger. Kids have already mastered this digital art form. The record is 85 words per minute by a kid. It's faster than a typist record.

How we fall don't define us. What defines us is how well we rise after we fall. Do not continue to fall victim to this new era digital zombie apocalypse. Rise you and your loved ones above it and digital detox, not further indulging into digital space zombie land. Take a tool or two to take with them to detox and guide digital world for tactical use, not recreational abuse. We also will tackle all of those troubleshoot and teach you how to spot and build your recovery areas.

I took the time out to manually write this book pen and pad the prehistoric way to help people that's lost in hypnosis in the digital space indirectly. Also to lead by example to make sure I do not use no digital devices and detox to write this book with effective methods, challenges, and solutions to help you snap back into your sense and reality where you actually owned and loved your own space or creative space. So I secluded my surroundings and gave up things like Sunday football games to master self, temptation triggers, break habits, and fall out of daily patterns. This book I will also show you how to put yourself in a digital quarantine and do a digital cleanse, offering you sustainability and to develop role model of thoughts and actions you want people to see that you push. What can you do to stop the conflict? Are you the culprit or victim? Also contagion transmission of such a digital hypnosis or disease is an influence on the mind or emotions to continue to relapse to reward and alter your mood with digital enhancement hacks.

It's similar to the effect of coffee stimulus hacks. It gets you up and going. Afterwards to crash down and feel worse and lose all of your sudden burst of energy, motivation, and your happy mood. That is until you have another cup or false sense hack. Your brain is wired to signal you to indulge again and again. This is no different than the digital space. It's actually worse because it's an epidemic norm of digital consumers lost, zombified in the digital space. It's not too late to detox.

- Chapter 4 -

"Addictive Visual Cues"

Everyone is acting and reacting the same. It is not that people are thinking the same. Even though people are not thinking more as they usually do because of new digital era. It is because of your addictive visual cues. Not in a movie, but in your everyday life, that's triggered by all the digital space, usage, and devices. Reliant on digital visuals that trigger your senses.

A visual cue is something you see or perceive and it instantly triggers an action, thought, or emotion usually. It can enhance, alter, or reward your perception with instant gratification, which also hacks your sensory, too. Digitally stimulus is a false sense, but this is what we attach to, further captivating us into digital oblivion. Then the addiction and addictive behavior becomes apparent. This is where you pay attention to your patterns and actions to recognize your addictive habits and digital usage.

You must take responsibility. You indirectly immediately cue things, just like we can cue happiness by triggering it from joyous things we see, hear, or memory.

The internet gives everyone a voice, their own voice to be heard or made. Also to establish an identity and digital platform or alter ego. People want to add to their Insta stories on social media platforms because everyone else is doing it, too. Again, neglecting daily priorities, needs, and values over digital imagery of your digital bio, profile, and identity.

Digital norms and edevices dictate your everyday life. Each time you did something digitally and it worked 9 out of 10 times, so you say yes, it works, and you can do it again, thinking you actually have control. Well, you don't have control and never had control, just an illusion of control. Do not put off living, dreaming of becoming and chasing an optical digital illusion.

In this chapter we will teach you if you first commit to digitally detox to recognize it, fix it, reverse it, and detach yourself. Become self-conscious of trigger cues, usage, habits, patterns, and addictions. Reclaim power to shape and shift your life. Become dedigitalized.

Now, just because you have a visual cue does not mean you have to act on it. Same thing with a thought process, too. Meta-cognition we can observe our visual cues and thoughts, but don't react to the triggers. Quantum physics. If you react to triggers, it will engage you, making you want to seek immediate reward and stimulus. Implicit memories in the body and universal points of nutrient body. Your body is recording all emotion reaction stored in tissues and visual cues for same conditions. Both hemispheres in the brain working at once.

Addiction is also a genetic disorder. Some genes are genetically different, or passed down of addictive traits from parents or previous generations.

However, we can develop our own adaptation. The brain still has a reward system. Axons release dopamine—chemical addiction neurochemical number one dopamine chemical of salience (survival important) signal warning for future.

Dopamine is more of a chemical of drive of want versus pleasure. It's not actually pleasure, it's the actual need and craving that triggers dopamine and addiction. Difference between who likes you versus who wants you. Synapses push high surge of dopamine surges in mid-brain reward system. They support own illusion of importance and value. Then you default the action.

Mobile phones and edevices cause dopamine-releasing chemicals to surge, still pick up addictive behavior. Instant gratification and convenience or profile status and images is their content media life versus real life.

The communication thru electrical and chemical in your brain hemispheres. A presynapse sends a signal, and a post-synapse receives cell. It's dopamine molecules and dopamine receptors to protein. It can create euphoria when it's overloaded with dopamine and changes hardwire of your brain.

However, dopamine surges help the brain learn. Prefrontal cortex is responsible for thinking, planning, loving, rational, and decision making. Mid-brain does not think, gets us through the next 15 seconds. Tells us to eat, sex, survive, etc. Usually the prefrontal cortex has the mid-brain in check.

Addiction can hijack mid-brain survival system addiction, creating a substance or engaging in a certain behavior like social media or gaming overload usage, etc. Addiction cannot be used as excuses. The brain will change, rewire brain, and cause you to see different.

It needs time to adjust back to normal. Be patient and do not engage in addictive visual cues triggers long enough to help your brain heal. Also resist cravings and temptations by steering clear and avoidance of certain edevices, apps, and gaming console or social media platforms.

This is how you recognize it, fix it, and detach from it. Law of neuroscience says nerve cells that fire together, wire together. Facts, so challenge yourself to recognize visual cues and avoid reaction to triggers of addiction cues.

Reverse it by creating new thoughts and something positive to look at in that space and you'll start changing your emotional energy to joy. Put a humor cue or happiness cue in place of sensory digital addictive cue hacks. New thoughts change your life. Also feed your brain natural dopamine, like exercise, food, or even sex. A natural risk and reward center, not surged dopamine hacking your senses to give you intense euphoria leading to want more and immediate addiction.

Change the way you think and act by the knowledge you retain and discipline yourself to apply daily. To change is to think and change environment and our brain.

We think to our environment, predictable patterns of perceptions. To change is to break our thinking of our reality in being we create automatic program to not deal with reality. You must force your brain to fire in new sequence, new wills, and to think in new positive ways. It will problem solve naturally and know better judgment between what's right or wrong as long as you put natural and healthy things in front of it. Stop feeding and fueling it with poison directly and indirectly. You have to be aware and very conscious not to keep feeding it into the digital world and become hypnotized in a zombie digital glued state. People perceive reality with emotions, virtual reality, and all the new digital social norms now. You must recognize this and detox, after you take time out to break and break away.

You have observations and naturalistic observation that's great at describing behavior but not explaining it. Hypothesize but do not over-generalize. See how one trait or behavior is related or correlates to each other. Sudden words and behavior change. How to recognize behavior traits by not manipulating them or being in denial and further distance in them.

It's visual affirmations, too. You can apply the method daily. Your eyes need to view it for your mind to believe it and intake it to subconscious perception create into a reality. Seeing is believing. Most effective affirmation because some people ignore themselves and others tell themselves habitual lies. However, the truth needs to be sought, and is way better when seen. Like the mirror effect when people look in the mirror, sing in the mirror, and speak to themselves in the mirror to play into the persona they want to become.

You must alter your belief, create good habits, chase discomfort, and overcome digital temptations, usage, and struggles. You cannot buy skills or experience, you have to learn it and earn it. Work towards it daily.

If you lack energy, put all devices down and regain positive energy, eat and work out or on something to take your stress out and shift your mind to positive.

Enhance your perception and intelligence daily. Take charge back of your life. Be conscious of your mortality and what you perceive. Fix yourself and pay attention to yourself. Do not actually identify yourself with digital norms, footprints, or social media platforms. Those dating apps and profiles is not your spirit. Your fear you fight. However, you cannot fight what does not exist.

At least enjoy what's going on in your head, if you cannot enjoy what's going on in the world. No matter what you do, you always going to want to do more. Reclaim your power and sensory natural stimulus. Focus needs to be inward, not outward. Please do not be a victim, user of abuse further by society digital space take-overs.

It is like the human naturally can detect a trillion odors by olfactory receptors to allow us to smell. Just like the brain has glucose for a natural state to enhance. Well, imagine you looking at augmented reality of a garden in a gaming system or digital program and all of a sudden you start actually picking up scents and stimulating your sensory organs. This same hack of false reality are the same actual acts we are falling into the loops of being addictive to it indirectly. You can detox digitally and get back on your innate correct path. We don't want to lose human genome coding blueprint trait or alter our gene pools with offspring born dependent on digital new norms, A.I., and machines versus people teaching them hands-on.

Even though you can learn from Google and YouTube, they cannot teach human nature or behavior and decision making.

They don't have human spirit, they are just programmed to do all commands of their duties and aids of placements.

However, you cannot stop bringing things new to people that they love, especially electronic. Do not digital relapse, instead use your digital devices and platforms as tools versus enhancements to your visual cues and sensory. Like the virtual reality headset black box, it can be used to work out and increase your health, not to overindulge excessive hours.

We becoming desensitized from all the digital consuming on our timeline. Mind power turns to willfulness, a different frequency and vibration after you level up and open your inner dynamics. You not in touch with reality, only your thoughts to reality, which is consumed and hypnotized by a digital world of electronics and programs that addicts and controls you. You must break free, understand universal principles that govern reality. You have fear, doubt, worry, insight, and inner directness. It hits our nervous system, it informs our thoughts, your energy, the template, evolutionary impulses. Must not let mass digital marketing machine control you and later your true identity and belief systems. Inspired, pain, growing and developing external natural motivation. Reprogram your mind, become aware, and tell your mind what you shall do and want. It contains infinite potential. From a quantum level or spiritual level inside of you, it's something lacking. Beware of what your surface visual cues is perceiving.

- Chapter 5 -

"Digitally Quarantine"

We have covered the problem, cause, effect, and solutions. Now we will go over effective methods that practical to push. Visualize the digital problems and habits you suffer from with all possible outcomes to push symptom versus focus on illness. Motivated forces, willingness to do what is difficult, to do what is right. When you have habits, they weapons to grow and create mental energy, your focus and stamina.

This effective methodology is crucial to your digital detox process with a digital cleanse. Cleanse digital manipulation usage, self, and slate free. Free both let go and tie it to life-altering and threaten cause by doing a digital quarantine, a state of enforced isolation like it's an actual outbreak. Act as if you do not quarantine yourself, it will be life-threatening cause. A preventive mechanism, a period of which digital space is forbidden contact with mobile phone or edevices.

You don't have to psyche yourself out, just do it. A little time sequence daily if you cannot go cold turkey. If you give up your cell phone or internet and social media platforms, you will be successful. Shut out the world for 2 hours to start daily practice to create new habit and a ritual to get better and quarantine for longer periods until you become efficient and dependent. Remember easy choices, hard life; and hard choices, easy life.

Digital literacy is a lot easier to implement these days. People are deeply interdependent and social medial influencers. Have online superpower and reach, increase by likes, views, and sharing with friends and family going viral. How we deal with it and play with it pushes us to look for digital validation and chase cyber fame. Even if you be more savvy player and play all angles, Silicon Valley and tech companies still control it. Influencers versus followers rule online. Also you are what you share. Digital dementia, digital deterioration, short attention spans, and becoming reliable.

A behavior is belief-driven. Your digital patterns can be broken and you can create new patterns, adapt, and teach. Put blocks or restrictions on your edevices, social media, etc., and time frames. Certain things you use daily that occupy your time too much in a digital space.

Not just a bait-and-switch, instead cultivate extreme resilience and eliminate stress of digital space. Get more done out of time by digital quarantine, more focus on work, family time, and self time of all real productivity. You need your energy level high to go into quarantine initially and each time to fuel your productivity and detox success.

It's pleasure, meaning, and engagement that hold you in a hypnosis state in the digital consumptions. However, you must understand and grasp once excitement and enthusiasm wears off, you lose interest because you do not feel it has meaning. Now reflect on your digital hangups going thru it gives meaning.

You cannot sit around playing on your mobile device being sentimental. Do not be archetypal of all digital consumers. Quarantine, detox, rehab yourself. Your sentences do not have to end with an exclamation point or semicolon to it. You have to be dedicated and committed to practice, carry out, apply, perform, and challenge yourself. Work at quarantine for a few hours daily where you cut all devices and notifications off or put up to relax your mind, reset, and rebuild self. Do it repeatedly to become proficient.

Do a lifestyle change and style with a quarantine digital detox method, isolating yourself from all digital devices and platforms. Digital detox to get rid of toxins during the process and addiction habits. You push yourself and normal functions also during this process and go thru temptations, digital withdrawals, and malfunctions. However, you must fight thru it and for it, if you want it and do not bend or break back in from your quarantine daily ritual time stipulations. Alter your process to suit you best until you can regain sustainability over your digital usage, life, and become dehypnotized.

Be receptive, available, and open to change and conquer your ego. Fear of change is the ultimate virus why people relapse after their detox. You must indulge in detox and surrender to the next stage of betterment to detox digitally and live your best life. Think about longevity, and bring yourself back to mortality versus digital identity and virtual reality. It is not a biohack or a pill to digital detox or therapy; it simply is within you and your will to use these effective methods and detoxing practices like quarantine from gaming, dating apps, social media, and all digital over-usage. Same way like a keto diet cutting out on carbs, with digitally quarantine you cutting out all digital forms secluded for an amply gross period until it's organic.

When you post a selfie, it posts a mirror image that's actually backwards. Same image people and imagery see themselves in the digital cyberspace in a backwards perception manner that boosts their egos and digital persona and profiles. This same digital syndrome is what you need to reverse and detox from.

Your transparency will help you and people transformation. Especially in your household and the people who you influence and follow you. Nobody is perfect, but it does not mean you have to accept defeat with a losing attitude, being afraid that you cannot win from your ego inner nagging dialogue.

Subtle energy which is what 6 sensory is. 6 sensory people know we are spirit, look at the world different, connect, and create. It's always a sparkle in eyes, smile, and moving and dancing with vibrant energy. Whereas a 5 sensory person who lives out of left brain, one who stops energy flow, and lives in fear of the ego. You cannot be afraid to leap in life. Only thru experience you learn life lessons and how to shift energy and turn off and on that ignition switch in your head.

We can only progress to the energy around us and absorbed in us. If you not enthusiastic with energy going into detox and digitally quarantine within and that vibrational energy, you are bound to relapse or fail the detoxification process. Also if people do not feel that same vibrational energy flow projecting out within, they won't help themselves or you back with positive energy as motivation. You influence people and move people with your vibration and positive energy, too.

Be intentional about digital detoxing, and bring positive change of betterment in your life back to the basics of innate human nature and sensory. Peak performances and energy from start to end of your day.

It is the way we react to circumstances to who we are. When life gives you a lemon, make lemonade. If you really want to gather honey, do not kick over the beehive, which people are kicking over the digital beehive and ego signal fear to get stung if they detox or take a step method approach to digitally quarantine for a few hours a day successfully. Trust me, it's only the digital hypnosis effect, you won't actually get stung by digital bees unless you on a virtual reality band headset or gaming console. The woman/man who goes further is the one who is willing to do the work, hard work, obstacle courses, challenges, and dares to change for self-betterment. You sure can. I believe in you for even just attempting and taking time out to read this book or listen to it on Audible.

Positivity and awareness is an effective mental and physical antidote to digital detox poison and digital addictions. Negative content and thoughts poison our perception and body. First the spirit becomes hypnotized, then the mental becomes sick and stagnates in repeat automated mode. Then the body and sensory organ biohacks become altered and enhance highly for addictive traits, creating new detrimental patterns, constant stress, impatience, ill humor, and choices souring the body rational decision making. Poisoning cells and senses with false augmented reality.

It's not possible to alter other people's minds for change and commitment. However, everyone can begin and practice by challenging themselves to digitally quarantine and give up their 10 top apps for a few hours and all edevices per day. In this way act as a model for others in their digital detox transformation. Do not look for only external happiness. People change when they ready and want to change life directions for themselves. You have to want it for yourself.

Remember that inner dialogue of nagging self-doubt and self-sabotage that you have not mastered or managed. If you really accept that there is a vibrant sensation in you that is attracted to the digital disturbance thru the principle of resonance. You move from impotence to power and can contribute something to the solution and digitally quarantine self. We accustomed to react to circumstances, events, and people. For us to take control 100 percent responsibility for everything that comes in our life means that we leap from reaction to action. You may actually discover your superpower and a trait to master during this digital quarantine detox stage isolated from the consumer world of electronics. It also will put you in a euphoria meditation-like state of a clear mind to achieve and focus in our daily or life goals.

Quarantine is a solitary confinement, can be therapeutic, neurotoxic, control for contribute variables, and restore hedonic tone in brain. All-in-all beneficiary and helps your memory hippocampus retain naturally versus relying on smart edevice to store it for you.

Put normal dopamine during this quarantine period. Natural competing rewarding activities. Take out daily digital addictive dopamine spikes. Daily "dopamine load" assessments.

Please engage in healthy norm activities to reverse. Even sleep and drinking is a natural detox, and a panacea in this digital apocalypse. Distress comes in different ways and digital pandemonium. The digital detox and effective quarantine method is not just your big win or accomplishment. It is to look for what you were truly missing or didn't work prior.

If you take time out to commit each day to turn off gaming console, stop binge watching, put up all edevices, and log off line by cutting off your WiFi altogether and challenge yourself to achieve a daily goal and long-term goal. Find your calling, work on life goals and dreams, pick up a book, exercise, spend time with loved ones, manually study and read. You can even spend time digitally quarantine outdoors in wildlife or simply walking a pet in the park. You are not meant to sit and slouch in place all day, eyes forever glued to a digital screen of choice. If you advance your time, you can advance your mind. You as a human being are meant to move, walk, travel, and grow.

- Chapter 6 -

"Content Creators vs. Content Consumers"

There is a huge split between consumers and creators. It is inevitable for a major divide in the next 5 years. The future wave of the digital world and technology is rapidly advancing. It's a competitive marketplace consumer filled. It's all about instant gratification and convenience of who can come out with the next big thing first. Any labor-saving devices or any digital technology suitable for personal comfort and ease is all included in the new creator's wave for the consumers over-indulging. They count on consumers and target them specific to a niche consumer column. They know people are hypnotized and self-programmed to go after new digital products, apps, programs, and advancements.

If you have a smart phone or tablet that meets all your needs and you paid $600, in 6 months a new device comes to the marketplace and you spend another $800 for an additional camera or more gigabytes for faster spend, you truly you did not need it and set you back financially in a bind. Being a digital zombie, you don't think because the addictive cue is hypnosis and triggered to surge overload amounts of dopamine reward instant gratification systems time and time again.

In this book so far we have gone over the problem, cause, effect, solutions, and methods. Right now we are going to focus on values. How to reverse-engineer your inner conflict and create value out of it versus continuously getting consumed by it and letting the rich buy and pull your value you out by dangling new consumer digital projects in front of your screen. Just think about it: When was the last time you saw a non-advertisement commercial or ad? When was the last time you saw a free commercial to help people detox, live healthy and organic, or exercise place for free? I'm not saying you cannot find regular groups that add real value of health, detox, and consciousness, but they do not put these groups, places, or organizations in front of you for a reason. Look at all the unhealthy fast food, alcohol, vaping ecigarette products they advertise around the clock nonstop. This is another reason the digital detox is so valuable to your awareness, mainly because it puts a conscious filter back into your subconscious and disciplines your ego of no filters of reality.

Your subconscious has known for a long time that you are not in harmony with your conscious values and experience an inner conflict of misplacement with no true inner design guidance of approval and structure. What can you do to stop the conflict? What can you do to create a new you? Do you want to really be a consumer or a creator? Are you the culprit or the victim? Are you afraid of new method formats, structures, and challenges? It all starts within you, because you hold the key to all your answer and question. However, you have to be willing to submit to self-discipline and interlock your inner conflict so you do not further self-sabotage.

I will show you focal points how to create value and how to set up value for your creative content versus being a consuming product victim. Also to be clear so you are not confused, I am not handwriting this book for you to stop all digital interactions. I know it's not possible nor do I promote you living under a rock. My sole purpose is for your eyes not to be glued to the screens, but used by the digital medium what it was created for: quick hacks and modern-day solutions, not to overexert usage of self-gratification to where it has hooked you in a hypnosis state to where it's causing you to slip in the digital matrix, lost from true reality, where your workplace and performance and family is being totally neglected indirectly. Once you are hooked, you cannot turn it on and off with your phone. They do not have digital detox rehab clinics to help people or kids with this digital epidemic.

However, you have to really believe and know you can reverse it. To prevent from becoming a content consumer, become a content creator of any sort, not just on a digital platform scale. If you spend time watching, liking, sharing, and purchasing every new digital product, then you are definitely a content consumer. No need to be in denial. I will show you how to mend the huge consumer-versus-creator split. The big question to really ask yourself is: Do you want to be a content creator or a content consumer? If you choose creator, then you must apply yourself in the content creator realm. Even if you a speaker or teacher, you need to understand how to further advance and create your content and build it up. You will add value from you and to people to share their learning and helpful experiences. It don't have to even be in a digital realm.

First write down every action it takes to make your dream a reality. Invest, deposit your seed in soil, and it will come out. Create a vision to solve, set a big goal and build it, communicate and organize and collect and retain your own data to be successful on what works and what people like and want, versus not and wasting product, inventory, and costly time.

Creative content and ideas is if you have an itch, scratch it and go after it like the inventor of Uber founder saying if with one button on a smart phone I can call a cab. Content creator with quality and knowledge, engagement succeeds higher production values to create.

Creativity is putting your thoughts and ideas into practice with value. Some aspects is problem solving—6 thinking habits, brainstorm. Find a medium that really moves you and your interest. Find things you good at and love. Different things incite our energy. There are practical things/tactics you can use to spark your creative thinking. Discover your element.

Create and connect with your audience, with amazing performance adding everyday values to people's life and implementing practical tools to assist them and engage with them, too.

Success is studying the formats and closing in the gaps. Influencers create value. Monetize consumer attention.

You need to platform yourself and show the world why you great, or what you make great. The value you bring to the world, products, brands, solutions, changes, accessibility, convenience, etc. Fast track on demand understanding effective marketing strategies.

Basically bring or introduce something new to the world, a new system or way, new venture, product, brand, innovation, etc. People are thirsty with curiosity. Then you control your creation realms and rules to have people and laws of physics bend to.

Entrepreneur is a sport and speed is key element of success and acting on it. If market not booming off your product, brand, or service, it's time to move on. You got to know when to move on and let go, on to the next big thing, project, or service. It's like a new gold rush with digital consumers, how big companies you love use your data and trade like oil. The true cause of split. Use it as tools. Again, it is not used and meant to be abused. This is a forewarning for the future. You will be digitally consumed further loss in the matrix, wishing you would have taken the time out to apply yourself and digitally detox timely.

How do you build your audience? Remember, you do not have to be online to do it effectively. The youth and people want to copy off heroes they idolize. Love talent and something they can do as well, or try to emulate. Entrepreneurs are creative and hungry by nature. It's 3 ways to capitalize off channel/brand with ads, brand integrating, selling content to platforms off your camera, like photos with 4K camera. They are always looking for new images to purchase. It's many tips you can learn but to create is to carve your own lane.

Learn to use digital platforms as tools to work for you instead of you working for it, further building its data. Remember A.I. is about mimicking and surpassing human capabilities. Algorithm is a procedure for solving a problem, especially in mathematics or computing. You are your own algorithm. You do not need Alexa and A.I. to further have you digital reliant and relax when you can be creating in your own space and platform by reversing it.

World is now built from creating and implementing. You must have hope, inspiration, motivation, transformation, and transcendence. Is it easy? Can it work? Can I do it? Yes, if you willing to put in the time and work, it will and can. Those are the first 3 big questions you ask yourself.

Now, how to capture the perfect product or testimonial that people want to hear. Tell what life was like before and after/now. You'll start attracting people to add visibility to you and continue to build this ciphering concept.

Discover big lever, know your avatar, perfect customer, cultivate heroes, use master class to make your products fit. You can even use free digital platforms and tools to create and connect with audience, people, investors, and celebrities. Start a movement, trend, challenge, competition people can follow and want to be a part of a building community base. Maximize on content and capitalize on your creativity to its prosperous fruits. Create a huge brand to market where everyone goes, something new that stimulates or innovates and caters to the world.

Jeff Bezos was a garage start-up on Amazon at first. He started with an innovated problem-solving thought process and put it into action by acting on it and applying himself to scale his company. Look how people use a product, how they search online, what they searching and order. You can take a feature people using and make it bigger or better that people can use better usage and innovated. Create and discover a world of content pioneering, antagonizing the status quo. Icons of engineering and architecture. You have a divine intervention always.

You do not have to be an intellectual innovator. You can build a team of people who can work for you, or automate processes and use ecommerce sites, too. Social media you can use as a way to monitor and engage, connect with people/customers, and see what they want, into, like, and what's hot. Use social media to harness your business as a tool, not just posting ads.

Remember, what problem is your business, brand, or product solving? You have to prove the concept, scale, and market profitable. Good content, repetition, practice, role play, and accountability. You need to think different, be around people who think different, and big without a limit or digitally consumed and zombified. Associate with people who pull you up, not down. Do not listen to them or pay attention to them. It cannot be no digital distractions or time for play in a digital consumer space. If you truly want to be a content creator versus content consumer, I suggest you detox from digital abuse usage further.

- Chapter 7 -

"Break Yourself & Kids Out of Habits"

A habit is when the body becomes mind, and to change it you need to turn the mind back into the body. Needs to work together, from thinking, to doing, to being. Move to the habit of being that.

In this chapter I will show you how to break yourself and kids out of habits and falling into digital patterns. Set restrictions for self and kids. Remove its harmful influence. Digital new norms of excessive screen usage and abuse is only a habit of addiction. I'll show you how to spot patterns and look for behavior shift patterns. First we need to be able to address habits as a whole and redirect the attention back to the inception of the mind and perception. The triggers of patterns and habits.

Let's go straight to some confidence and pillars of self-esteem. The practice of self-responsibility. Self-acceptance.

Practice of living conscious. Improve what you can, accept what you can't. Practice of personal integrity. Practice of self-assertiveness. Finally the practice of living purposely.

Do not ever rely on your bad habits. There is a such thing as good habits, like working out reading, meditation. You can even possibly turn a bad habit into a great one and reverse-engineer it, too. Like if you spend way too much time on social media platforms scrolling or trolling, you can reverse it to a plus side. The tools, structure, and engagement to be successfully on social business to further drive value. Emerging positive opportunity and influence online with social brands and communities. Get people to adopt new policies, ways, etc., from old habits, versus making familiar and people to understand. You can even reverse your bad habits to focus on a good specific acute target problem-solving market to add positive value.

Remember value exists in the plan, but more so in the process of planning. Requires near-term commitment for long-term commitment. Making a commitment to break habits, work harder, and out-work the competition of digital distracted world. Focus on your strategy, plan, end goal to accomplish and stick with it with perpetual daily dedication.

Start working on one habit and goal to break first in the morning. If not, it will get pushed off and you would relapse, getting nothing done or conquered.

Now this is how your mind of habit works and triggers. Every time you have a thought, you have a chemical, so you can feel exactly how you thinking. Then brain signal to feel the way you think, the way you feel, and feeling becomes the way we think.

Then we create these habits and personality traits and being. That loop of chemical conduit becomes being. 20 years of suffering, the body gets enough information to become mind and that's created habit.

You modify your receptor sites. The body tries to tell the brain a message thru spinal cord to release the chemical to recondition all it's trained for. And signal subvoices saying you can start fresh tomorrow thru fast track of nervous system and slow track on other system.

We teach them a different agenda. Like remembering a phone number, your conscious cannot. However, your body can because of repeated pattern you automated. You can reverse this, break habits to good ones and new health patterns. Personal your action, habit, and patterns, then create new experiences with new thoughts and new self.

This is an example given. If knowledge base freeze in your mind, like for instance, the doctor tells you that you are paralyzed in your arm, you would tell me, no, you cannot move it and it's paralyzed because the doctor told me so.

The same status quo of feeling and thoughts condition your brain and body to think sick and alter your DNA. It's the external environment that we push that. When you push genes to produce proteins and reproduce, to do cheaper protein. So by telling your body distress, it signals protein in areas and minus in others, like grey hair or hair loss.

A whole new learning, new information, pay attention, and instructions. Then you repeat it and will have new brain cells for new health habits. Memory helps maintain them, so do more memory exercises daily. New patterns, new thoughts, you gain new circuits and wiring. What do you mentally rehearse, i.e., think about, and who you are as a physical, and actions all day.

They create a mind just by thinking about it. Do it every day with a new experience and thought process to originate new habits. Send new chemical signals neuro glue cause connection, more stronger grow and enrich. More circuits in place to send signals. The reality is the brain has a server of 400 billion bits process info every second. However, we only deal with 200 bits of it.

In breaking bad habits for you and your kids, you must first understand the attachment of 4 key things to conquer and be successful, which is the body, time, awareness, and environment. You must begin to retreat from the environment so it does not distract you from breaking bad habits.

If you put your kids or a person in an enrich environment, they will do other things, healthier, and social mingling. Yes, you should put time stipulations on your kids' online usage, gaming console, and binge watching. You cannot come home from work and give your kid a tablet just to keep them occupied so you can get lost in your digital space indulging, then expect to be habit free. Instead you are actually influencing the kids versus shutting off all edevices and engaging with them, schoolwork, dialogue, and interactions. You cannot just set up a restriction from downloading an app to put time stipulations on your kids' phone or tablet and expect it to work. The kids will simply use their text messages, games, and movies or special features download on their devices. You can't expect for your kids to change when you keep putting tablets, gaming consoles, and mobile devices in front of them and try to monitor their usage because you already created the habit and hypnosis to the new digital era. You must replace the kids' devices with things to do and places to go, like engage in youth programs, outdoors, sports, playing instruments, etc. There is a whole bunch of things they can do to keep them busy and off those screens all day long.

The different environment and placement for you and the kids is pivotal to habit breaking and changing the patterns for great traits and new habit pick-ups. We need to find different therapeutic environments to facilitate the breakage of bad habits. Stop boxing yourself and kids in. You cannot continue to be stuck zombified in fear of failure in the creation process of new enrich habits. You have to step in your kids' life further, no more disconnect. Do not do cold turkey or your kids will build direct resentment. Break their habits into new habits a little at a time with new practices and events a few hours per day until you can wean them off edevice dependence.

They did research with the lab rat model where they put a lab rat on a boxed-in environment with a heroin access panel. Then they placed the same rat inside a different enrich setting environment with other rats. It was successful off the heroin and engaging with other rats and breeding. So our environment should not be toxic. If so, we can never implement true change to kids' habit nor our own bad habits.

Your frontal lobe makes up 40 percent of your brain. People turn off circuits of who they are, losing time and space, creating new circuits in frontal lobe and new self. To get people going from thinking to doing because they do not apply simply because they do not believe it or feel like it, excuses.

When you change, you break all your habit agreements for your environment. If you share same experience, you share same emotion agreements, same chemical fire. Take what we read and learn and apply it to new experience to change. We began to change and alter chemical and brain. Then the brain is now organized ahead of experience.

It is a great balance between head and your heart. We learn new habits, choices, and develop a tool for it. Realize you have to change the narrative in your mind to get different outcomes and help break you or your kids out of patterns of over-usage and bad habits. Organic things and thoughts leads to organic choices and habits.

When you in thought process of creating a new habit, you get happy. Remember creativity is a joyous activity because you falling in love with what you creating, especially organic habits for you and your environment. You are inspiring and chemicals driving circuits. Use elusive emotions. Your body will be freed up from restricted space and bad habits or bait trap triggers of addictive patterns and procedures. Mental rehearse, the mind should be doing thinking before action. Think to doing always and work on this effective format for solution and problem solving all around, not just bad habit forms. This methodology can be applied to aid you throughout your whole entire detox digital process effectively.

The cost of inaction, do fear settings emotional, physical, and financial, etc. Get out of that digital bubble and write down on paper a list of all your good habits and bad habits of you and kids on a separate column. Then see what it is for you to work on with visualization to work on and daily to break. You have to cut off all edevices and take a time-out quarantine from digital world. Challenge yourself, act like you lost your phone versus your mood when you actually lose your phone and shape-shift your thought process, break patterns with your visual affirmations on walls, paper, etc. Self-impose pressure, push it further and process all your momentum, then disconnect your mind to digital dependency to reconnect into reality of independence of you and your environment.

For your kids, especially if they are gamers, not mobile with lack of energy, you must challenge them, too. You cannot just simply not pay your WiFi and take their gaming console because they find hot spots for WiFi or go over friends' or classmates' houses. We, the parents, are to disengage. You have to yield them with an effective solution to reverse. Where you let them engage in gaming, programming, coding, design apps, or send them to schools or course, they can be involved in a positive organic habit. You can't stop it, but you can help put them in a structural gaming environment where they doing more working than time sitting around gaming. Their minds will be occupied, too busy trying to problem-solve, design, or create special feature in a gaming community to be a part of. They will not have too much time or energy to continue to binge gamer mode with a new habit or organic.

- Chapter 8 -

"Troubleshoot"

We all have troubleshoot areas, some hidden, others is more directed and accumulated. Egos, imperfections, failures, cannot stop or turn off, losing focus, people, work, family because of obsessiveness in troubleshoot areas. You need to learn how to turn focus on what really matters.

Do you offer self-sustainability, develop a tool that meets the needs of troubleshoot area? People and problems that we perhaps see as our foes are really our best friend, adversity challenges, because they show us where we have to work. Now the big question to ask yourself is: Can you spot or discover it without other influenced triggers? What things do you use to contribute to the troubleshoot problems and justify the behaviors? New methods, challenges, exercise overcoming obstacles.

Can you identify and imply effective solutions in those areas like your online usage of time, content, dating apps, social media scrolling, and being in freeze mode like a brain freeze being caught by same hang-up pattern built in systematically?

You must use different angles and have precise tactics, like divergent thinking, tackling problems head-on with a dive-in mentality despite fear of outcome. Extract more value, understanding, knowing, learning, and growing. Also importance, find and truly successfully identify your niche troubleshoot problematic areas. Reform, reset, regroup, and amend. Have standards, accountability, and boundaries. Use it as a tool and develop a new skill set equivalent that find, signal warning that something is wrong, broken, or hazardous to health and cognitive well-being.

Virtual reality comes into real-world reality once we create and trend it, just like ice bucket and bottle cap challenges, which is the number one troubleshoot area we suffering from and hard to admit and identify. It spirals into us like the going-viral effect. It's contagious. Your network flow, info, connections, and support shares between people physical or virtual. If it's a lot of views, you too insist on clicking on that image or viral video to see what the world buzz is about, too. We affect ourselves and work life in the realm of the digital space, never thinking to troubleshoot or detox. After all, there is no place to go to yet to digital detox effectively or dezombify yourself glued to screens. This is a syndrome.

How can you put an effective system into play? Teach and connect an example or a framework how to be a successful model. Implement problem-solving timely concentration where you focus time, resources, and best possible ways to simplify solutions in a real effective manner. Identify your biggest risk, find out and eliminate fears, doubts, worries, and problems to be solved. What motivates and triggers them. Learn when they start to know how and when to stop them. Learn where they are and you can be your best you and best all-around performances daily. The psychographics and divine discontentment, it brings horizon creative impulse. Enable you to discover your troubleshoot triggers and how to troubleshoot in that area disruptive while finding your own big lever, vision, and discontent. Who or what you must fix, get under effectively. Even if you do not like something, you can still enjoy time and space after you troubleshoot.

Find your true life quest and inner blueprint structure design to reflect and direct outward. Do not fall into the digital social realm of people personal profiles as this actual identity in reality. A prime troubleshoot problem in the digital space going unsolved and recognized.

Inflection, the act or result of curving or bending. Be a quick adopter, and acting quickly, tackle those troubleshoot areas with self-accountability.

Obsessed versus observant. You can be very observant, not excessive because it triggers obsessiveness. The ego who wants to always be right and in control. It's really not in charge. Ignore it, do not imply it with reaction or counter-reaction. Refrain it, do not let it win again and again.

Now, how to spot, stop, and switch shift your mind is to troubleshoot by looking at it as being bad for you, poison, or life-threatening, etc. Then change or alter your perception that causes you to depend, crave, and have loss of your senses.

Self-discipline, self-control, self-conquer, self-love, self-build, self-help, self-awareness, your cognitive skills, and rebuild all skills. A strategy for what you see is what you want, get, is mainly what's in front of or around you and influences as an optional choice and a visual cue for addictive triggers.

Another effective solution is to increase speed of implementation for troubleshooting areas. How long it takes to apply. They absorb and implement at lightning speed. The rate you take action. Next is the ability to take action when you do not feel sure of it, uncertainty. They do not waste time, they take action. How much you value your time. Do not waste your time. Do you waste time on social media or lost in the digital space and wonder why you cannot effectively troubleshoot and fix those life problematic areas, especially in digital realm? Or do you make things happen?

If we can catch our vibrations and shift them when they bad, then we can detach and rewrite those bad hot spots. Think what timelines you need to cut out versus the ones you use, and make new ones. Time travel intervention shift and move effective. Shifting timelines you shift the field and energy around you, not just inside. Release limiting structures that don't serve. Seal your field. Transform your troubleshoot distortion into a gift. The core metrics of reverse-engineer a troubleshoot process within yourself.

Maximize your full capacity. Event plus response equals positive outcome. The structures is not ours so we dissolve them, command to dissolve it. Tackle your troubleshooting accurately. Let it go, release it. The limited structures was imprinted in our field and no longer serve you.

Tune into your body wherever it feels it and see the color that form or object and simply request it to shift and remove troubleshoot areas out of your body, elevating the surging problems. Activate it in every cell in your mind and body, allowing the mind to do its job. Let it move you with signals and triggers to change and shift problems and evaluate new energy to tackle it. To manifest of your desire, a specific code, or divine code. Surrender to link your mind to a positive image to respond to words and change. Let them know their value, importance, and special inner powers. Now invite highest self a third energy to come in and show your highest version of you and higher self-connection. Allow it to shift into heart and head to lock in troubleshoot. Then know this version of you will be available at any time you activate it. The strongest vibrations at the temple and seat of your inner instincts. Integrate it in your head and heart, then dismiss hang-ups that clinch or freeze you in those perpetual life areas.

Remember, your intentions first to tackle any external or internal event. Shift, readjusting, and revaluation of self. A full support of your higher vibrations and conscious thinking.

Release all distortions, higher structures, self-doubt/sabotage system that fuels your ego. Then return to the focal point to fix the matter, not wasting time on the recurring matter.

In that event and reality you choose that. And with so much self-appreciation, gratitude, and shift yourself into now. Then see the timelines shift in troubleshoot.

Now address your internal traits, too. Replace energy with positive affirmations, mantras, using it over and over as your daily ritual. Also visual triggers like images and pictures you tie to your words help. Like if you say Saturn and you automatically see a picture of rings, simply off words you trigger signals to cue pictures in your head. Vivid words can lead to vivid pictures. Then pictures can help you limit or leave a bad trait pattern area. However, your addictive triggers or trigger words, you shouldn't use words that trigger self-doubt, emptiness, and hopelessness. Like just, hopefully, if, try, and should. Which all set you up for failure or to binge and relapse because you already planted a perpetual seed of self-doubt to self-destruct mind and all behavior.

You must be able to manage self before you can manage anybody or thing else. Remember that your rule of mind is every word created from thought, blueprints and stays in head. Your mind is too clever, when people like something they remember it. Whatever you feed your mind, it feeds you. If you have it in your head, you can put up the edevices and dedicate a few hours a day to digitally detox successfully despite temptation triggers, then it shall be done after the mind creates it into a reality.

Once your mind realizes something, it reacts to make it possible. Whatever you imagine defeats real logic. Logic does not work, emotion does. The mind don't care if right or wrong, good or bad. It lets it all in. When you say to the mind, "I wish, I hope," versus you saying, "I will do this, I am this, I do this, I got this." All of our mind's words activate faster than Google naturally. Your brain is already a supercomputer. You are too reliant on digital computer that you can focus your mind and trigger natural response time and problem-solving troubleshoot features.

Rely on your good organic habits and daily rituals, not motivation and inspiration, because it does not always do the trick or hack, and gives you the push needed to spark your cause to go.

You must really dive in it, adapt it quickly and you will adopt it, and tackle it, ride waves, making progress in troubleshoot.

Decide and go. Trust facts and systems in you and around you. You will truly be amazed at surge and capacity, and ability to naturally get in and go.

Also identifying your triggers, make a list, write down what you feeling. Then what you not feeling. Mind think is nature of thought. Key is for natural peace, total control over self and reactions, not other people. Look for blessings, having natural energy, being natural self. Having an accountability buddy to help you with troubleshoot, body language, behavior, over-usage, and addiction. Practice acceptance, do not judge people or beat yourself up if you cannot successfully troubleshoot effective areas correctly and fix the problem or spot arising issues. It is a practice method of implement initially to develop with each repetition.

Lastly, remember to always reverse-engineer. The faster you consume, the more you want, and like binge watching faster point speeds. Pushing your attention span, addiction further craving, and focal point harder.

- Chapter 9 -

"Boost Willpower"

Your willpower is the most important tool to digital detox or in life, period. Your will is your true intention and always stays in accordance with present tense. Will is an adjective. Your initial inception and creative process, and your push power.

You cannot do a quick hack to boost your willpower, like a 5-hour energy drink that simply stimulates the sense temporarily. You have to enhance your willpower by your own self. Self-actualization is what's needed in will. Passion, purpose needs to be stated with intentions to spark your willpower. Everything gets meaning once you give it means.

Your will to win needs to be your same to start and will to execute, whether a problem or a desire. Most people start off defeated and don't stand a chance to win or finish their conquest because they detach their will from the very beginning.

Just because you are willing to do something does not mean will is behind it, too. Determination and willfulness is not your infinite will, nor boost your willpower immediately. Your will is not just your power of controlling your actions or emotions. However, it is a mental innate power.

When dealing with subconscious mind, the greater conscious will effort, the less the subconscious response. Remember your will forms a blueprint what the mind wants, and willpower ignites your blueprint. What you focus on, you direct your will to do it, and your mind will produce vibrant willpower boost to fire the action or fuel the desire to carry out.

Your will likes familiar and do not like what's unfamiliar. This is why some people do not fire or misfire their willpower. Or know how to boost it accordingly to the premise with intentions attached effectively. Your willpower works for you the more specific your intentions are. You must be clear on your intentions and objective for willpower boost to push thru or conquer successfully. Some people possess willpower natural organic to base their intent and carry out. However, you must master how to boost your willpower perpetually, igniting that switch to complete any task or dire obstacles. A lot of people go wrong by dreading a detox digitally, depleting their will before it can boost, divide, or conquer. Also ego becomes the enemy after you restore your willpower to master it. Do not get fixated and fascinated, else ego will grow and boost. So any obsessive or unhealthy preoccupation or attachment.

Before you attempt to achieve boosting your willpower, you must first will the action in order to achieve it. Even visual cues and recognitions are anchored by your will, too. Tap into mental will, cut out cognitive distractions and triggers. With boosting your willpower, take steps backward, a time-out to reflect, and appreciating nothing digital, then your universe can proceed in harmony and reveal new unexpected solutions to boost willpower if you try it out.

The full thrust behind motivation and inspiration is your true will. Your willpower steers your drive, even when you out of gas on E. It will get you thru anything and take you to any place. All you have to do is trigger your willpower, and it will deliver. You have to clearly state your intentions to your will so it can attach and activate the command. It's a big difference between commitment and dedication. Just because you commit to an act does not mean you are fully dedicated, especially if you experience turbulence and hit some rough spots. That's when you access your will to the act but did not activate your willpower boost to push your will thru full throttle.

The scenario is similar to professional athletes pray before a game or match-up and they state their intentions to win and bliss from the Creator with protection. Then all of a sudden they cannot hear the fans or crowd, they are too busy focused on their opponents and their drive from behind their willpower. That intent and beforehand act simply pushes your engagement and enables you or moves you to shape and form your command. Do it with embodiment. Embrace it and let it flow thru you naturally, and you will feel a different sense of energy and push, a different anxiety solution. Helps you prevent distressful moments due to lack of will or poor performances because you cannot deliver on key or timely.

It is a difference between mind will and your emotions. Learn feared with your ego and emotions will push your inner nagging voice will derail you from using or activating your willpower and boost it further when needed. It will tell you that you will never detox or get to the top of the mountain, even if you have one more step to climb. That last boost and push needed from your willpower will be defused or altered from your ego and emotions pulling you back down into neutral drive or even into park, which when you are stuck in park, your willpower is not shifting, it's sticking into place, misfiring or not firing at all. This syndrome is called complacent.

Accept your emotions, let them move thru you, not out of you to control your will or other areas to box you in. You cannot just get comfortable in one place in your life and be happy with yourself because it just works and fit into one area. However, it lacks in other areas but you are too complacent and comfortable where you at without leveling up and pushing yourself to want more in life and enable your innate growth process in life, too.

If your will is to not stay on social media, binge watching, gaming, or dating apps, you must connect your willpower to switch at any time. Some people can trigger it and switch to quit cold turkey at the snap of a finger. That's how powerful their will influence to push their drive. You must create a positive will and put a conviction on it. Your will is not meant to make you comfortable, it's to simply ignite and drive you. How can you use your will in your transparency or platform to push and serve you thru discomfort? It's not no secret or hack, you must push will on demand.

When you speak it's your perspective or emotional response, it's not your will. You can exhaust yourself, not your will or boosting your willpower.

You can try exercises, for example, like remembering your passwords or phone and PIN numbers. You do not have to challenge yourself to do it. Just insert your willpower and ability to trigger memory to boost. It's like using Google and it fetches your query searches out of the cloud data stored. Your mind is actually better than the cloud because it stores lots of intel that's tailored and cultivated for your survival and existence. Your mind will be attempting to trigger your memory storage department, and body will try to emulate by entering passwords or numbers automatically to get lucky and break its dire task to communicate with brain function of memory, which signals distress because you cannot remember it. However, the thing behind the drive that's pushing mind and body to trigger memory on cue is simply your willpower. You can train your will, you have to simply activate it, turn it on beforehand. So before you do anything, commence your willpower. The more you do this, the more natural it comes to where you bestow this in you beforehand in all life endeavors successfully.

During my digital detox I took the time out to manually boost my willpower with a card game of memory. Each morning I would use 36 cards out of the deck, place them on the floor to pick out 18 matches. Then I would challenge myself with time and speed, pushing my willpower and boosting it at will. Even after I eventually used the full deck of 55 playing cards, I could match up the complete deck in 8 whole minutes total.

It's not cultivated compassion, attachment of illusions, or unscripted acting. No, it's simply will of purpose and intention. It's law. Whereas, the unconsciousness push you on a deranged path and moment of reckoning. It's not about a new convert to a system, it all begins with you, not your heart or spirit, but to transform your innate will to activate without thinking twice or distraction from ego and self-sabotage.

Focus on conveying your willpower. Work at it. Segmentation and identify what, when, and where you need to boost your willpower from. If it's temptation, digital distraction that you do not think you can fix or get out of those bad habits, you have to keep inserting your willpower. That's the life force behind the commandment. You can do this, it's never too late for change.

Some of our wills were programmed and template of parents and society, where we do what parents bestowed us and from their own will in us, and we adopt it as our own. So once you reach adulthood, your free willpower is altered or simply dormant, where it does not move to the right trigger cues. To teach yourself to reprogram your will, you first have to know your will you own is truly an adoptive will. Next you must activate assertive willpower usage in smaller actions before you trust and believe your will to push the drive button on bigger actions you want accomplished.

Meditation, self-actualization, with time out to really isolate your mind to strip all ill will attachments, and really find your true will by shutting off that impossible ill-willed voice inside. The same voice that tells you life is hard to do this, or you don't have a will to do that. You need to ignore and learn to reach out to that switch to tap back in to your willpower. Reconnect the loose or broken wire because it's highly possible within your human nature. In your fight-or-flight mode wired in you naturally, sometimes your ego can play into the way of your receptors by fear, where your willpower or boost simply do not reply or fire accordingly. If you teach and reach to your mind to turn off all self-doubt that's disabling your will to fire and push it to fire on demand successfully on key.

Sometimes memories of trauma or abuse can come back to us and make it feel as if we are reliving them and shutting our willpower down, too. When that happens it's important to try and return back to the present, which is the state your will dwells in. One way to do this is through controlled breathing.

Controlled breathing not only keeps your mind and body functioning at their best, but it can also lower blood pressure, promote feeling of calm, and help you relax. Breathing exercises can be something you do every day or you can do these when you feeling very heightened and triggered in any moment.

Practice try inhaling slowly through your nose for a count of 5, then exhale through your mouth for a count of 5, too. If you have not tried breathing exercises before, start with just inhaling and exhaling for one minute. Work your way up and push for at least 10 minutes a day. It takes some time and practice before you can do controlled breathing for 10 minutes at a time. You can try any one of the breathing techniques best for you. Close your eyes to do them in a quiet place, sitting down or lying down all works. Focus on your will.

- Chapter 10 -

"How to Digital Detox"

To digital detox successfully you have to break into new habits and create new patterns as a daily ritual and push yourself to the daily challenge. Even if you relapse and break your digital detox for that time period of usage and digital dependency, you must not accept defeat and get back on your detox. You cannot let your addiction reward system continuously win and beat you out.

In this book so far we covered the digital problems, cause, effect with effective solutions and methodology. We went over values, digital quarantines, breaking habits and creating new ones, troubleshoots, and boosting your innate willpower. To some people it sounds easier read than done.

However, if you put all these elements into practice daily rituals, it will help you transcend. Enhance your daily performances and get back to your human nature and natural senses versus hacks of virtual reality in the digital space. Taking on social media identities, work identities, and identities that's been placed on you that you feel you have to play into the image of other people's perceptions of you versus your own true identity and self-perception, which is buried down in layers under others that you consistently adopt and take on in the digital space and your workplace. Most of us are not aware of all the personal habits, traits, patterns, and bad habits we take on from others. During your detox process it will help you shed all those false layers and identities you picked up over the years.

Your conviction has to be a real cost to challenge. You need willpower, motivation, to rattle any form of complacency you have. Your life is about serving you first, then others. Do not be compelled or compromise your mission to detox from digital distractions you thinking you can't live without. You can finally stop scanning apps and texting while driving, which is illegal, and have energy and time for workplace and loved ones daily.

The desire you trying to become boundless, through the boundaries. Comfort and convenience happen naturally, not bliss of self. Commitment prepares you to meet obstacles and overcome downfalls and temptations during detox. They prepare and expect to win, combined with persistence. It takes real intention, focus, repetition, and practice daily to reform a successful new habit and detoxification, a fundamental requirement. When you operating a sophisticated machine, you need to know how to properly work and control your mind, willpower, emotions, body chemistry, and energy. Learn to teach your mind your own self-download program in self-awareness and actualization. Your elements.

Be very intentional in your detox for changes you seek. They won't be immediate changes or the instant gratification you are accustomed to in this new era digital space. What you care about makes you happy and insert your will to succeed at it in full effect. You need to grow yourself organically in order to grow outside of the digital cloud. Remember your good habits and the techniques you use for strategy. Fierce competitors refuse to lose and trained to win.

You can even go on a digital detox remote retreat, get away isolated with couples, kids, family, or partnerships to get back to their basics and senses. That real intimacy, family time restored, or even the kids playing outdoors, building their immune systems up naturally, all being deprived of elements.

The detox process you have to challenge and push yourself. It's awareness and daily rituals and practice to bestow in your mind. Self-therapy with a method of triggers and awareness to quantum leap often succeeds within a few minutes. 100 percent responsibility and power to take responsibility means understanding that you dispose of the free will decision to choose your reaction to actions. You can set up mental triggers to substitute like joy and attach a vibrant joyful visual behind it, too.

Digital consumptions, digital overloads, and hypnosis of top 10 apps you cannot live without daily and hourly. How to differentiate what's best for you and way to detox daily and quarantine from them all. How to evolve, scale, fuel, feel, move, unlock, morph your mind, give your innate access like Google but better. A computer program or device could malfunction or crash; your mind will not, though. How to push your normal mind capacity, how to use more percentage of your brain, pushing the average 5 percent to disrupt the human status quo like the monk ancient practice method capabilities. You must detox first to enable yourself into a higher level to soar and platform.

If you asked the average teenager old enough to drive, are they responsible, they will say Yes, they feel entirely responsible simply because they do not text and drive, they use their Bluetooth responsibly. Which they own it and feel proud and very confident, sure of themselves. Also more screen time is now linked to caffeine and coffee, so basically people are double-dipping on overdosing both, feeling dopamine surge overload. It's an outrageous problem.

Find a way to attempt new things manually, something you like to pull your attention and focus point off your mobile phone or tablet and add 8 hours to your day. It sends signals to your genes to say you should be here and give you reason. A true-life cause to be better and strive for greatness and detox.

Detox is ultimate life hack to get your derailed life back on norm track. You can be connected with something without having an actual vibe and true connection. Do not sell your will-to-win succeed in your digital detox as bad as you want to breathe. Your breath and breathing is always with you from beginning to end, whether distress or failure and success. Your breath feels every emotion if you learn to control it, navigate it. Always go to root and cut down the weed root to your mind or heart, else it grows and becomes a total weed.

You can learn from social memes sharing and harmful content on social media platforms by reversing it instead of bullying, trolling, or hurting some cyber behind that screen. Instead simply spread peace, love, joy, and compliments, making people's day. You can do this literally off social media in reality. Honor people, friends, family, and things. Say thank you, have manners. When you compliment people, it goes a long way and positive energy to their day. People need to feel appreciated and valued in person, not just validation in a virtual reality space. All that does is further aid their cyber identities and false sense of reality, not real self.

Before we get into some more effective detox techniques, you must remember to see your resistance and look at your split, the inner critic that holds you back self-sabotaged. All practices you do should take you back to that split, of truth your reality as one. A journey within, integrate, and marry your truth, will, and authentic self organically. Also remember that all these digital and virtual reality identities and any name label is merely imagery of delusional consumers in a hypnosis zombie state of mind. You cannot be a label or a title, only you. Be the best you with all of you and detox successfully to lead by example to others.

First I want to go back to positive affirmations technique. Positive affirmation and visual affirmation or positive statements are reprogramming tools to our subconscious mind, which push our thoughts to actions. Positive or visual affirmations should fit in your particular troubleshoot areas, insecurities, emotional distress, willpower, etc. A positive affirmation should interrupt the pattern of getting stuck in harsh beliefs by replacing the negative thought with a loving one. Instead of looking in the mirror and say, "Forget my life," look at yourself with strength and stand up in perfect posture and say instead, "I can detox! I will digitally detox successfully." You can even tell yourself you are loved and supported, you are strong, courageous, brave, and could achieve anything humanly possible. You are very powerful. Your mind will grasp it and bestow it by switching you into gear. This is not easy if you keep being pulled into digital world distractions. You just need to digital quarantine yourself. Then choose any affirmation you'd like to practice, saying it out loud daily or whenever you need to switch your mind self-doubt, emotional distress, negativity, and lack of will and self-control.

Then it's back to your breathing techniques. Remember you can choose whatever breathing exercises that fits you best and help enable you to detox daily rituals. You do not have to take on difficult free diver technique. You're not holding your breath, just you attempting to control your breathing to relax and calm you and sense down.

You can try another breathing technique by putting one hand on your chest and the other on your stomach. Take a deep breath in through your nose and try to fill up air through your chest and stomach. Repeat this deep and slow breathing pattern 6 to 10 times per minute, and try to work your way up to 10 minutes each day. Then take notes of your heartbeat and feel it calming down to give yourself a compliment for your great work taking care of your temptations and digital distractions to take back control of self.

Now let's jump into another technique of mindfulness and meditation. Mindfulness is the art and science of paying complete attention to the one thing you are doing at any moment.

Meditation and mindfulness are self-care tools that can be practiced wherever and whenever. Just like the breathing exercises and positive affirmations, they take body and brain back from the negativity, distress, and distractions.

Meditation is a practice that allows the mind to exist in a calm and natural state.

Meditation in practice is to start by sitting down and allow yourself to become very still, relaxed and alert. Try to focus your attention on one thing. It can be anything you choose. However, 2 great places to start if you're new to meditation are either focusing on your breathing or on a word or phrase called a mantra that you repeat over and over for the duration of your meditation. Some examples could be, "I am in control of my lovely life and detox" or "I am loved and have the power of free will to boost."

Sometimes people prefer to make sounds that don't have a meaning but are soothing or chakra auras, like making a noise as you breathe out or humming. You can utter, chant, it's all okay. As you do this, your mind will wander, which is okay, too. Try to allow these thoughts to pass by like a flying bird, or you can shoo them away mentally like a pesky fly. You get over 50,000 thought processes per day. You cannot stop your thought process, but you can pop that thought bubble and dismiss it.

Your only job when you practice meditation is to bring your attention back when it strays from your object of focus. Even if you find yourself falling asleep at first, it's not extreme, that's okay. When you practice, try to remember to stay focused on breathing, relaxed, still, and alert.

Meditation and mindfulness can also include other techniques and activities, like body scanning. A body scan allows you to pay attention and notice each part of your body. This can help you reconnect to parts of your body that may still hold distress, trauma, and painful memories that's difficult for you to think about.

Start by lying or sitting in a comfortable position. Pay attention to your body. Start at your toes and move up your body to your head. Focus on tightening each body part and muscle group as you move up your body. Then release it. As you release your body part or muscle group, allow yourself to feel it getting heavy and relaxed as you let go of the burden of carrying it.

Another technique you can do in your detoxification process is wake up in the morning before grabbing your phone, checking emails and notifications or jumping right to your edevices, is give gratitude. Show thankfulness and appreciation for life, your life, your will, spirit, and energy to awake and start your day off. Gratification challenge every morning and at night before bed. Do it as your daily detox ritual as well. Then you can write down manually what all you are thankful for, what all do you love, what your short- and long-term goals or daily goals are. Also you can write down what best advice would you tell yourself 10 years ago? Try it and apply these techniques.

The next technique to your successful detox is a guided meditation/visualization. This practice is like meditation but you are imagining or visualizing a story instead of just a word or a sound. Man people will visualize a relaxing place and happy environment or the process of healing happening. Sometimes people will tell themselves a favorite soothing story as they visualize it happening. Maybe you want to visualize healing by imagining a ray of light coming to you and touching your body wherever it hurts, bringing you a warm glow and the feeling of safety. Maybe you want to imagine yourself with a loved one, making a favorite meal or place together. Think of something soothing that allows you to feel calm and at peace.

Next is praying technique, if you religious or not. If prayer is important for you, it can be a great way to integrate mindfulness and meditation. The next time you pray, be aware of straying thoughts and calmly bring yourself back to your prayers. If your prayers are physical in nature, become aware of the movement of your body as you pray. Think about how your hands feel when they move. Do you feel graceful? Do you feel strong? Energy or powerful? Make your prayer take up your whole body.

Now let's use a reflecting technique. If you are having a day where your thoughts seem very fast or very scattered, it can be helpful to describe your day to yourself. Include small things that you did and give yourself credit for all the work you put into surviving the day. Like today I woke up, I gave gratitude, and pushed positive energy into the universe while stating my clear mind and intentions for the day. I did my breathing exercises. I opened my eyes, I stretched my arms, and I got out of my bed. I made my bed. I washed my hands and splashed water on my face, etc. This kind of detailed description can help you to feel centered, and it can remind you of the many things you have power and control over. The things that you choose to do with your day, like open your eyes or stretch, those are choices you make for your body, and you deserve credit for them.

Now let's get into a grounding detox technique. Grounding is an exercise that helps keep you in the present moment and in reality versus virtual reality and digital identities. It can be helpful in managing overwhelming feelings, intense anxiety, or nerves. It can also help you regain control of your mental focus from a place of intense or high emotion. Grounding techniques can also help bring you back to the physical space where you are. When memories of trauma, distress, temptations, and digital distraction makes you feel a certain way or outside of your body, these activities can bring you back. Just like a live wire needs to be grounded.

Here are some grounding activities to try out. This is called 5, 4, 3, 2, 1. Name 5 things you can see in the room with your phone off; 4 things you can physically feel against you; 3 things you can hear right now; 2 things you can smell right now; and 1 good thing about your self or 1 new thing about yourself.

Next is questions. Ask yourself questions to help bring you into this moment. Where am I? What day is it? What is the date? What is the month and year? How old am I? What season is it? This is an example. You can use any questions you wish to ask yourself. The whole point of this activity is to get you back to you, reality, and a snap-back to your natural senses.

Now let's jump into the description game in your digital detox. Plant your feet firmly on the ground. Physically hold an object and try to describe each detail of it out loud, like you wanted someone on the phone to be able to see it. Try this with a comforting object like a blanket or a favorite shirt. Now try it with an object that is rough.

Next get creative, whether it's actually writing, drawing, or making music, like I did in my successful digital detox, too. Expressing our story or experiences can be an important tool to help us let go of emotion, pain, distraction, temptations, and trauma. It's therapeutic in life and vital in detox.

Creative expression can use our whole body and brain, and this helps us to remove distress and trauma from where it may be stuck in areas inside of us to reform. When we create something, we have the option of sharing our art with our community. Whether it's a beautiful drawing or a letter, turning our pain into creativity can be a powerful experience, both for us and others.

Next is make music. Music does not have to be made with a traditional instrument. We can make music using our bodies, our hands, our voices, and items like pens or pencils. You can try to make a familiar tune you love, or you can write your own piece. Music moves spirit and everything around you with vibrations and drums.

Next detox technique is our physical exercise/movement. Sometimes our experience cannot be captured on paper or on camera. Use your whole body to express what is inside of you. Try wiggling your toes and fingers, stretching different parts of your body, shaking out your arms and legs, or walking around. Notice the rhythm of your steps and breath, and use this natural beat to create movement.

Then let's do a rare, now outdated technique via letter-writing. Letters or cards, sticky notes at workplace, or to people for empowerment and positive energy vibes. The art form of writing and being off your edevices feels brand new and it's a crucial tool for recovery and creativity during your digital detox process.

Write letters to people who care about you and support or been there for you in the ups and downs of your life from day one. Write letters to your idols, your past or future self, people who have hurt or helped you.

In the letters, you can say what you wish you had known, what you wish you had said or did, and what you want to say one day. You can choose to send these letters, keep them, destroy them, or throw them away. It is the point of the act and therapeutic behind it which helps you in detox pull away from digital distraction to build back up focal points. You can even write yourself and send it, write down accountability and standards needs to be met, etc.

Next practice technique is a journal process. Journaling, document your daily interactions, accomplishments, tasks, important events, or whatever comes to mind at the moment. All while your mobile phone is off. Allow yourself to write freely without judgment. Let it all out and flow. If words do not come to you, use drawings.

Finally, reading. Read something new or reread something that makes you feel good. Don't cheat yourself, pick up a traditional book. The old-fashioned page-turning way, held in your hand, versus your handheld tablet. Memorize a favorite line and use that line to inspire you during meditation.

All these techniques you can do during your digital detox without any edevices. Time and divine intervention with self and space to build and grow, breaking bad habits and addictive behavior and pattern. All to assist you in your positive transformation and detox process. Do not be afraid to ask at least one person for support or help and to talk to when you need it. You must keep your will intentions clear to succeed in your digital detox not to relapse further or being a digital zombie permanently, lost in the digital matrix. You must remember to use it as a tool for you, not against you, to program you instead of you using the program. I believe in you, but you must believe in yourself and betterment.

I've now showed you how to digital detox and where to start at. The question is: Can you really put down your phone and digital detox successfully? Are you ready to detox? After you read this detox book, after 72 hours motivation and inspirations die down. Is your willpower strong enough to sustain you to actualization and follow this? Do not let your mid-brain addictive cue reward system trigger or tempt you. Nor let your ego fatigue and defeat you. Take the initiative further and step into your digital detox and get back on your natural human nature and senses versus reliant on virtual and augmented reality. It is a health choice, cognitive, and the way of life. Begin a whole new way, new world, new you, and digital detox.

About Author

Hitachi Choparazzi is a New York City native, by the way of Omaha, who is currently incarcerated in level 5 solitary confinement in Florence, SMU-Eyman Complex, serving an illegal sentence awaiting on Supreme Court Appeal to correct his sentence with time served. The error forces him to serve 2 years extra.

He is an entrepreneur, tattoo artist turned author. Also the sole owner of Chop-a-Style Publishing and Productions, and the owner of Chatmon Sr. Literary Agency. He has written over 20 books and including scripts to pitch to Netflix. All this while he was incarcerated to start his reform act.

Founder and CEO of Billion-Dollar Blueprint and the BDB movement/youth movement, an innovator entrepreneurship where he believes everyone has their own blueprint, like everyone has their own unique thumbprint. Based on 3 core principles—Education, Elevation, and Innovation—which he teaches the youth and people how to format and discovery key. BillionDollarBlueprintmerch.com

The face of lockdown society movement along with the voice of lockdown society movement. IncarceratedLivesMovement. com #ILM #BDB

"I do this for y'all. I love y'all, rep y'all, and believe in y'all! I won't stop giving y'all all the raw stories as God bless them in my head. I have a hundred of them up there. Anybody that has a hot hand, send me samples or any comments, suggestions to my FB, IG Hitachi Choparazzi or email: orders@ chopastylepublishingllc.com Chop-A-Style Publishing LLC and Productions. TeflonLuv!"

Hitachi Choparazzi prides himself on having his own signature Chop-a-Style where he freestyles all his books. They all rhyme with innovation and original storylines. He writes prequels, sequels, trilogies, and more. Does it for the people who love to read and for all those incarcerated in state, federal B.O.P., county, and women's facilities. FB,IG,Tiktok, Twitter, YouTube-Hitachi Choparazzi

Emails: Hitachichoparazziauthor@gmail.com
Billiondollarblueprintmerch.com

Chop-A-Style Publishing and Productions LLC

Other Books and Scripts by the Author

Non-Fiction

- How to Rap; The Elementary Teaching of Hip-Hop

- How To Tattoo & Start-Up Business

- How To Digital Detox

- How To Start-Up a Food Truck Business

- How To Stop School and Mass Shootings: Dear Parents

- Incarcerated Lives Matter: The Hitachi Choparazzi Blueprint

- How to Love

- The Switch: A Social Awareness Self-Help

- Nipsey Hussle Lockdown Society Dedication–Tribute

- If Trayvon Martin Could Talk; Injustice

Fiction

- The Eagle and Weasel (1-5 series kids' book)

- She Go! (urban novel)

- Reality Show 3D-HD (urban novel)

- Hot Thots (urban novel)

- Liqz (urban novel)

- Paranormal Whisper (horror novel)

- Pimp of Da Ratchets (urban novel)

- Pimp of Da Ratchets II Vegas (urban novel)

- Pimp of Da Ratchets 3 Orange is Da New Pimp (urban novel)

- Hitachi (urban novel)

- Penitentiary Pimp (urban novel)

- Weasel Society (urban novel)

- The Big Pep and Plucker Story-She Go! Prequel (urban novel)

Screenplays/Scripts

- Top Notch

- Hot Thots

- Pimp of Da Ratchets

- Weasel Society

- Million Dollar Games–A Secret Society

- The Eagle and Weasel (animation)

Available at Barnes and Noble and Amazon

Welcome to the exclusive lives of 4 extremely hot THOTs. This book will show you how to spot a THOT. From THOT tops to THOT flops, all the way to THOT Snaps and claps.

This book is the first-ever with a double twisted love triangle. Watch as Chicago, LA, ATL, and Seattle THOTs entwine at Coachella.

Some on fleek and some looking cheap, but they all cheat! They all commit aTHOTery with their THOTery acts, shameless.

Raunchy, with steaming hot sex scenes to sex swings. From wild threesome ménages, and twerking, to bare-it-all raw. Too hot! THOT gum pop...

This page-turner is an eye-opener to the very end, with a bombshell-dropping, shocking ending. The secret life of THOTs

Available at Barnes and Noble and Amazon

Billion Dollar Blueprint is a movement we challenge and inspire you to find your individual blueprint. Our mantra is "We believe everyone has their own blueprint like everyone has their own thumbprint". With these three core principles

Education

Elevation

Innovation

Hitachi Choparazzi is the founder and CEO. Orders available to support incarcerated businesses.

Orders available at: billiondollarblueprintmerch.com

www.ingramcontent.com/pod-product-compliance
Lightning Source LLC
Chambersburg PA
CBHW060325130626
46553CB00003B/924